AMERICAN HISTORY BY DECADE

The

# 1940s

Titles in the American History by Decade series include:

The 1900s
The 1910s
The 1920s
The 1930s
The 1940s
The 1950s
The 1960s
The 1970s
The 1980s
The 1990s

AMERICAN HISTORY BY DECADE

# The
# 1940s

## Don Nardo

KIDHAVEN
PRESS™

THOMSON
————— ✶ —————™
GALE

San Diego • Detroit • New York • San Francisco • Cleveland
New Haven, Conn. • Waterville, Maine • London • Munich

**LIBRARY OF CONGRESS CATALOGING-IN-PUBLICATION DATA**

Nardo, Don, 1947
  1940s / By Don Nardo.
    p. cm. — (American history by decade)
Summary: Describes the United States during the decade of the forties, focusing on involvement in World War II, becoming a superpower, and the development of "pop" music and television.
Includes bibliographical references and index.
  ISBN 0-7377-1516-2 (alk. paper)
  1. Nineteen forties—Juvenile literature. 2. United States—History—1933–1945—Juvenile literature. 3. United States—History—1945–1953—Juvenile literature. 4. World War, 1939–1945—United States—Juvenile literature. 5. United States—Foreign relations—1945–1953—Juvenile literature. 6. Popular culture—United States—History—20th century—Juvenile literature. [1.Nineteen forties. 2. United States—History—1933–1945. 3. United States—History—1945–1953. 4. World War, 1939–1945.] I. Title: Nineteen forties. II. Title. III. Series.
  E806.N269 2004
  973.917—dc21

2002155398

# Contents

# A Decade of Sharp Contrasts

Looking back on the decade of the 1940s in America, the country experienced tremendous changes in just a few years. First, during the first half of the decade the United States was caught up in World War II. This was the largest, most devastating war in history. And waging and winning it required that most Americans make major sacrifices. As many as one out of every six Americans either served in the military or worked in businesses supporting the war effort. Also, many products needed for the soldiers overseas were **rationed** on the home front. These included gas, oil, rubber, food, and clothing.

In sharp contrast, the end of the war brought tremendous prosperity to the United States. Thousands of new businesses were created and jobs were both plentiful and better paying than before. Between 1941 and 1949 the average annual salary in the country nearly doubled. During the war people had worried about the future, which seemed uncertain. But in the postwar years they felt very confident about the future. Many wanted to live the so-called "American dream" of owning their own homes and raising children free from want. The number of couples who had children in the years following the war was so large that it became known as the "baby boom." (Today, the baby boomers, now in their fifties, make up about a third of the country's population.)

With so much prosperity, people rushed out to buy things they had not been able to afford in the past. In addition to houses, they purchased cars in record numbers. Also, luxury items and new gadgets were particularly popular. For example, many people who were eager to bring entertainment right into their living rooms took advantage of an emerging technology and bought television sets. The number of TVs in American homes grew from a mere six thousand in 1946 to more than 2 million in 1949.

New Yorkers line up to buy meat during World War II. Products needed for soldiers overseas were rationed during the first half of the 1940s.

## Then and Now

| | 1940 | 2000 |
|---|---|---|
| **U.S. population:** | 132,122,000 | 281,421,906 |
| **Life expectancy:** | Female: 68.2<br>Male: 60.8 | Female: 79.5<br>Male: 74.1 |
| **Average yearly salary:** | $1,299 | $35,305 |
| **Unemployment rate:** | 14.6% | 5% |

The change from wartime economy to postwar boom was not the only factor that contrasted the America of the early 1940s with that of the late 1940s. The nation also underwent an amazing military and political transformation. In 1940 the United States was one of about ten major industrialized countries in the world. Its status and power were not much different from Britain's, Germany's, or Japan's. However, by the end of World War II the United States was by far the strongest country on Earth. Its huge arsenal of advanced weapons, including the atomic bomb, made it the world's first superpower. As the decade ended, another superpower, the Soviet Union, was emerging. Clearly, the world in which Americans lived in 1949 was markedly different than the one they had inhabited only nine years before.

# CHAPTER ONE

# The United States Fights World War II

When the decade of the 1940s began, the United States had not yet entered World War II. That terrible conflict had begun in Europe in September 1939. Germany, led by Nazi dictator Adolf Hitler, invaded Poland. This prompted Britain, France, and other countries, who called themselves the Allies, to declare war on Germany. They also declared war on Germany's own ally, Italy.

At first the war did not go well for the Allies. Nazi forces entered Paris, France, in triumph in June 1940. Two months later, Hitler ordered bombing raids on England, which took a terrible pounding before driving the German planes away. It was only a matter of time before Hitler would send ground forces to capture England.

The British and other Allies desperately needed and wanted America to come to their aid. In response, President Franklin D. Roosevelt called for lending ships, planes, and weapons to the British. "In the present world situation," he said, "there [is] no doubt . . . that the best immediate defense of the United States is the success of Great Britain in defending herself. . . .We should do everything to help the British."[1]

"Everything" did not include entering the war on the Allies' side, however. This was because at the time many Americans did not want to get involved in the troubles of other nations. Instead, as much as possible they wanted to

President Roosevelt signs a declaration of war following the Japanese attack on Pearl Harbor.

keep **isolated**, or separate, from European affairs and wars. Many agreed with the famous airplane pilot Charles Lindbergh, who said, "We in this country have a right to think of the welfare of America first. . . . No foreign power is in a position to invade us today. If we concentrate on our own defenses . . . no foreign army will ever attempt to land on American shores."[2]

Only a few months after Lindbergh spoke these words, he and other isolationists were forced to change their minds. In December 1941 Japan launched a devastating attack on the American naval base in Hawaii. Because the Japanese were by now allied with the Germans and Italians in a pact called the Axis, the United States declared war on all three. America had finally entered the war that had engulfed the entire world. All involved knew the ordeal could end in only one way—the total defeat and **humiliation** of one side or the other.

# Target: Pearl Harbor

The main reason the Japanese attack on Hawaii was so devastating was that it was almost a total surprise. Relations between Japan and the United States had been strained for several years. But there had been no evidence that the Japanese were planning violent action against American bases.

The Americans had no idea, therefore, that a huge war fleet had departed Japan on November 26, 1941. The target was the huge American naval base at Pearl Harbor on the Hawaiian island of Oahu. The Japanese reached a point north of Hawaii on December 5. And early in the morning of December 7, 189 warplanes took off from their carriers and headed for Pearl.

The attack began at about 8:00 A.M. As surprised American sailors scrambled to defend themselves, one by

The USS *Arizona* takes a devastating blow as a Japanese bomb lands directly on its deck.

one their ships suffered heavy damage. Worst hit was the USS *Arizona*. Struck by a 1,760-pound bomb, it exploded in a giant fireball. The Japanese flight leader, Mitsuo Fuchida, saw it from overhead. "There was a colossal explosion in Battleship Row," he later recalled. "The shock wave was felt even in my plane, several miles away from the harbor."[3] All but three hundred of the ship's crew of fifteen hundred were killed.

When the Japanese attackers finally departed, they left behind a scene of awful devastation. They had killed 2,343 Americans and sunk or badly damaged 18 ships. They had also wrecked 308 planes that had been parked on the runways of nearby American air bases. Half of the entire U.S. Navy had been wiped out.

## America Gears Up for War

Americans reacted to the attack with anger and resolve. On December 8 President Roosevelt stood before the U.S. Congress and called for war. "Yesterday," he declared,

> December 7, 1941, a date which will live in infamy, the United States was suddenly and deliberately attacked by naval and air forces of the Empire of Japan. . . . No matter how long it may take us . . . the American people in their righteous might, will win through to absolute victory.[4]

Americans heard this call to arms loud and clear. People of all walks of life closed ranks in what became the biggest war effort by any nation in history. In all, more than 16 million Americans joined the military to fight in the Pacific or in Europe. Meanwhile, on the home front the country produced a staggering amount of war materials. American shipbuilders launched new warships at the incredible rate of one each day. The nation's assembly lines turned out more than 87,000 tanks, 296,000 planes, and 17 million rifles, while American farmers produced tens of millions of tons of food.

This massive output of war production changed the face of America almost overnight. Thanks to the effects of the Great Depression, many Americans had long been out of work. But now, suddenly there was work for everyone and the unemployment rate dropped from 20 percent to 1 percent.

An even bigger change was the appearance of large numbers of women and blacks in the workplace. Sending millions of men to fight overseas created a huge labor shortage. And many of their jobs had to be taken by women. More than 19 million women went to work, 2 million of them in defense plants alone. Blacks, who had long been treated as second-class citizens, also gained

A wartime poster urges men to join the military. As the United States entered the war millions of Americans enlisted to fight.

work and social status. A number of black women who had been earning only $3.50 a week as maids now made $48.00 a week in aircraft factories.

## The Brink of Victory

As American soldiers and weapons poured into the war efforts in Europe and the Pacific, the tide of the conflict

The number of women in the workplace increased as men left to fight the war.

began to change. In Europe, the United States and other Allies slowly but steadily destroyed the Italian and German war machines. The Allies landed in southern Italy in January 1944. And on June 5 they entered and liberated Rome. The next day U.S. and other Allied troops stormed ashore in northern France in the D day landings. As the Allied noose tightened around Germany, Hitler committed suicide on April 30, 1945. On May 7 Germany finally surrendered.

Meanwhile, U.S. forces drove the Japanese back across the Pacific to their home islands. The drive began when the Americans defeated a huge Japanese war fleet at

American officers sign the documents of Japan's surrender in September 1945.

Midway, in the western Hawaiian islands, in June 1942. Then the United States retook the many Pacific islands the Japanese had recently captured. Eventually, the Americans began to bomb Japanese cities. On the night of March 9, 1945, Tokyo, Japan's largest city, was almost completely destroyed.

Standing on the brink of total victory, U.S. leaders called on the Japanese to surrender. But they refused. To end the war, the United States decided to use a secret weapon it had been developing. At the time, few people realized that this weapon was destined to change America and the world forever.

# CHAPTER TWO

# America Emerges as a Superpower

By late June 1945 the war in Europe was over and the United States and other Allied forces had Japan surrounded. President Roosevelt had recently died. That left his vice president and successor, Harry S. Truman, facing a truly tough decision. Truman had two choices regarding how to deal with Japan and end the war. The first was for American and other Allied troops to land on and capture the Japanese home islands. However, the Japanese had already launched many suicide attacks against the Allies. It was clear that they would use this same tactic during an invasion of their homeland. A noted American general estimated the invasion would "cost over a million casualties to American forces alone."[5]

## Dawn of the Atomic Age

Truman's other choice offered the possibility of forcing the Japanese to surrender without the further loss of American and Allied lives. For several years American and British scientists had been working on a secret weapon. In fact, it was so secret that Truman had known nothing about it until he was sworn in as president. In 1939 German-born scientist Albert Einstein had told President Roosevelt that splitting atoms of **radioactive elements** would release huge amounts of energy. "This new phenomenon," Einstein wrote, "would also lead to the construction of bombs. . . . A single bomb of this type, carried by a boat and exploded in a port, might very well destroy the whole port."[6]

The massive effort to build the first so-called atomic bomb was dubbed the Manhattan Project. The first test of the new superweapon was held in a remote New Mexico desert on July 16, 1945. An American officer who witnessed

Albert Einstein informed President Roosevelt about the potential of atomic weapons in 1939.

the explosion later called it "magnificent, beautiful, stupendous, and terrifying." The sound, he said, was an "awesome roar that warned of doomsday."[7]

Indeed, a sort of doomsday soon came to two Japanese cities—Hiroshima and Nagasaki. On August 6, 1945, an American plane, the *Enola Gay*, dropped an atomic bomb on Hiroshima. When the crewmen later gazed down on the devastated city, one of them gasped, "My God, what have we done?"[8] Three days later, Nagasaki met a similar fate. After that, fearing total destruction, the Japanese finally surrendered.

## Dramatic Increases in Prosperity

"Little Boy," the atomic weapon that was dropped on Hiroshima, Japan.

Much of Japan now lay in ruins. However, with American aid the job of rebuilding began almost immediately. The United States committed itself to the generous and enormous task of putting the Japanese back on their feet and making them allies of the free world. America did the same for its other former enemy, Germany.

As Japan and Germany started to rise from the ashes, the United States emerged as the world's first economic and military superpower. On the economic front, Americans found themselves in the midst of the biggest boom in history. The American dollar was now the most valuable currency in the world. And the United States benefited greatly from exporting and importing goods to and from all corners of the globe. This created many well-paying jobs.

A U.S. sailor kisses a nurse in New York's Time Square to celebrate the end of World War II.

At the same time, millions of American soldiers, or GIs, returned home. They played a key role in transforming both the economy and society as a whole. Many of them took advantage of a special act passed by Congress in June 1944. Called the "G.I. Bill of Rights," it provided large sums of money to help ex-soldiers find jobs and get loans from banks to buy houses.

In fact, the need for affordable housing was immense. With so many people in their twenties and thirties returning from overseas, there was a gigantic housing shortage. Many former GIs moved in with relatives while they looked for their own places. A few smart builders soon made a fortune constructing entire neighborhoods of new

Children play in a suburban neighborhood in the late 1940s.

homes on vacant land outside the major cities. Schools, stores, gas stations, and restaurants grew up around these neighborhoods, which became known as **suburbs**. (Today, most Americans live in suburban areas.)

The G.I. Bill also gave ex-soldiers money to go back to school. The number of college degrees issued each year in the country rose from about 130,000 before the war to 430,000 by the end of the 1940s. Those with degrees were able to find better jobs. Because they made more money, they also paid more taxes. That gave the government more money to build huge road systems, bridges, schools, job programs, and so on. Thus, the children of these former GIs, the baby boomers, grew up in a much more prosperous and modern country than their parents did.

## The Cold War Begins

In addition to being the world's new economic superpower, the United States was also a military superpower. It had far more warships, warplanes, tanks, and bombs than any other nation on Earth. It was also the only country with the atomic bomb. Had Americans wanted to conquer the world, they probably could have. Instead, they used their enormous wealth and power to rebuild their former enemies and promote democracy around the globe.

Soon, however, a rival superpower emerged, one that did desire to dominate the world. The Soviet Union had fought on the Allied side against Hitler in World War II. And at war's end it joined with the United States, Britain, and France in overseeing the German capital of Berlin. The trouble was that the Soviets wanted to take over the whole city and push the other Allies out. In June 1948 the Soviets **blockaded** Berlin, or stopped all road traffic moving in or out of the city. The United States responded by launching the Berlin Airlift. American and other Allied planes flew

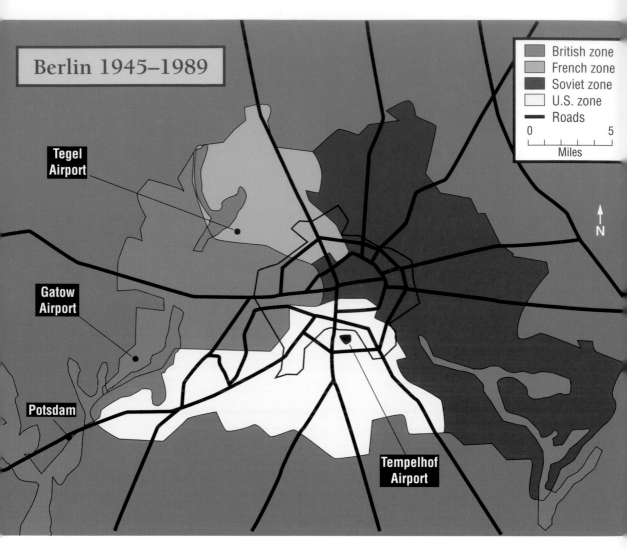

Berlin 1945–1989

British zone
French zone
Soviet zone
U.S. zone
Roads

0        5
Miles

N

Tegel
Airport

Gatow
Airport

Potsdam

Tempelhof
Airport

food and other supplies into the city so that the people would not starve. Seeing that their blockade had failed, in May 1949 the Soviets had no choice but to lift it.

A few months later the Soviets shocked the world again. In August 1949 they tested their first atomic bomb, which they nicknamed "First Lightning." News of this event sent a ripple of fear through America. Many people worried that the enemy would provoke an atomic war. Some American generals advocated using atomic bombs to wipe out every Soviet city before the Soviets built any more superbombs.

But President Truman considered that plan barbaric. Instead, he ordered the building of an even more destructive nuclear weapon—the **hydrogen bomb**. He hoped each side would refrain from using its nuclear weapons out of fear that the other side would launch its own. This marked the beginning of the Cold War, a tense standoff between the United States and Soviet Union that would last for many years to come. Americans were learning that being a superpower carried with it grave dangers and fear as well as economic prosperity and other benefits.

# CHAPTER THREE

# Music Makes Its Mark on American Culture

A merican "pop" music was the most popular and influential music in the world during most of the twentieth century. Certainly the music produced by American singers, musicians, and bands in the 1940s was no exception. During World War II some American GIs carried their **78 rpm records** with them overseas. They found that American big band, or "swing," music was already popular in Europe. They also found many young Europeans eager to hear the latest songs by American artists such as band leader Tommy Dorsey and singer Frank Sinatra.

Much of the music of the era was intended for people to dance to. The most popular dance of the decade was the jitterbug, which was fast, lively, and featured jumping and some acrobatic moves. American soldiers introduced the jitterbug to other countries during the war. And it became an international craze. Back on the home front, people who wanted to dance flocked to dance halls, nightclubs, country clubs, and other places that featured bands.

They also danced to music played by **jukeboxes**. These were big vending machines that played records when

A young couple dances in front of a jukebox. Big band music and the jitterbug dance became popular throughout the world.

someone dropped a coin in the slot. In the early 1940s, jukeboxes held twenty-four records. A big advance occurred in 1947 with the introduction of jukeboxes holding fifty records, each of which could be flipped over. That gave the customer one hundred songs to choose from. Thanks to live bands, records, and jukeboxes, 1940s pop music made a strong and lasting mark on American culture.

## The Big Bands

As the decade opened, the most popular music played by both jukeboxes and live bands was swing. The big band craze had begun in the 1930s with band leaders like Paul Whiteman and Tommy Dorsey. Dorsey remained widely popular in the early 1940s. Other famous bands of the 1940s were those of Benny Goodman, Count Basie, Artie Shaw, Glenn Miller, and Duke Ellington. It was Ellington

Swing bands like the Glenn Miller Band became an international craze in the 1940s.

who coined the famous phrase, "It don't mean a thing if it ain't got that swing!"

The typical swing band had twelve to eighteen players (though on occasion it had more). Such a musical **ensemble**, or group, was made up of trumpets, trombones, clarinets, saxophones, a piano, guitar, string bass, and drums. The leaders of bands and orchestras of earlier eras usually stood in front of the ensemble and kept the beat with a baton. In contrast, the big band leaders usually played instruments, too. Benny Goodman played the clarinet, for example, while Duke Ellington played the piano and Tommy Dorsey played the trombone. Sometimes the band leader or another band member played a solo while the rest of the band backed him up. Many bands also had full- or part-time singers for vocal numbers.

The swing sound most often featured an appealing **melody**, or tune, with a driving beat, or "riff," played under it. The songs played were both slow and fast. Usually the band alternated between slow ballads, for dancing "cheek to cheek," and fast "jump tunes," for doing the jitterbug and other wild dances. Despite these similarities, not all bands sounded the same. Glenn Miller once said, "A band ought to have a sound all its own. It ought to have a personality."[9] Each band strove for its own special sound, therefore. Miller's own band was known for having its clarinets play the melody, while the saxophones and other instruments added a colorful background. Some of Miller's greatest hits were "In the Mood," "Chattanooga Choo Choo," and "Tuxedo Junction."

## Solo Singers Become Stars

Swing remained popular in the late 1940s. However, music in the second half of the decade was dominated by solo singers, many of whom had gotten their start with the big bands. Bing Crosby had sung with Paul Whiteman's band, for instance. Frank Sinatra had sung with Tommy Dorsey. And the great black singer Billie Holiday had sung and recorded records with Count Basie and Artie Shaw. These and other singers eventually became stars by putting out singles and albums of their own. In addition to Crosby, Sinatra, and Holiday, the most popular singers of the decade included Dinah Shore, Perry Como, Peggy Lee, and Kate Smith.

Of these singers, Frank Sinatra was easily the most popular of the decade with young people. His smooth-voiced romantic sound went over especially big with teenage girls. Often called "bobby-soxers" (because they wore ankle socks nicknamed "bobby socks"), they swarmed Sinatra at all his public appearances. Many **swooned**, or fainted with joy, when he began to sing. This happened so often that newspaper writers began calling him Frank "Swoonatra." Needless to say, Sinatra enjoyed many big-selling hits in the 1940s, among them "Nancy with the Laughing Face," "Saturday Night Is the Loneliest Night of the Week," and "I've Got a Crush on You."

## Bebop and Rhythm and Blues

Even as Sinatra and other solo singers topped the record charts in the late 1940s, black musicians pioneered two new music forms. The first, bebop, grew out of the songs of some of the smaller swing groups. Bebop was not meant as dance music. Instead, people went to nightclubs and bars to watch and listen to the performers play. The ensembles were small—usually a piano, bass, drums, and a saxophone and/or a trumpet.

Also, bebop was more complex and difficult to play than standard swing. Often, the musicians would borrow

Frank Sinatra fans are giddy with excitement as they wait to see the singer. Sinatra was the most popular singer of the 1940s.

a melody from a popular song and use it as a starting point. Their main technique was to **improvise**, or invent new ways of playing the tune as they went along. Usually the piano, saxophone, and trumpet took turns playing large numbers of notes very quickly while the bass kept the beat. The result was a fresh, jazzy sound. Among the leading bebop musicians of the 1940s were Charlie "Bird" Parker, Dizzy Gillespie, Lester Young, and Miles Davis.

The Dizzy Gillespie Band performs during the 1940s. Gillespie and other black musicians invented a new style of music known as bebop.

The other music form introduced by black musicians, rhythm and blues, was based on traditional blues music. Blues tunes of the early twentieth century were usually performed by a solo singer backed up by a piano and sometimes a string bass. The songs were slow and the words expressed deep emotions and feelings. As the name suggests, rhythm and blues pepped up blues songs by giving them a rhythmic beat. Pioneers such as Louis Jordan, Muddy Waters, and B.B. King added amplified guitars and had the drums, rather than the bass, keep the beat.

At first, bebop and rhythm and blues were called "race music" because only black musicians played them. However, many white people came to enjoy them, too. And having a mixed audience helped break down social barriers. In 1949, for the first time rhythm and blues songs were allowed to be listed on the national record charts. Soon, white singers would begin recording their own versions of these songs, giving birth to still another pop music form—rock 'n' roll.

# CHAPTER FOUR

# Television Captures the American Imagination

Music was not the only kind of entertainment the American public enjoyed in the 1940s. As in prior decades, going to the movies was widely popular. And playing and watching sports remained important national pastimes. However, in the 1940s these entertainment staples were joined by a new one that quickly captured the public imagination. To the delight of many, television took the concept of radio a step further by supplying pictures to go with the voices and music heard on the radio. For the most part, television was still a novelty in the 1940s. At the time, few people realized that it would quickly transform the lives of nearly all Americans.

## Experimental Televisions

The rise of television in the late 1940s was sudden, swift, and huge in scope. Yet this invention, which came to be called TV for short, was not new. In fact, experiments with the concept of television date back to the late 1800s and early 1900s. These early experiments toyed with different ways of capturing visual images and broadcasting them from one place to another. The approach that eventually proved best used a glass tube and a beam of electricity. In 1923 a Russian-born American inventor named Vladimir Zworykin introduced such a tube, which he called an iconoscope.

Another inventor, American Philo T. Farnsworth, used the same approach as Zworykin. On September 7, 1927, Farnsworth, then only twenty-one, presented the first public demonstration of an electronic TV. One of the men who had invested money in the project asked the inventor, "When are we going to see some dollars in this thing?"[10] So as a joke, the first image Farnsworth broadcast was a dollar sign.

Experiments with television continued. In 1939 the RCA Company demonstrated TV broadcasts at the New York World's Fair. One showed a speech by Franklin Roosevelt, who became the first U.S. president to appear on TV. That same year witnessed the first televised baseball game, between Princeton University and Columbia University. In contrast, as

A young boy eagerly watches a baseball game on TV. Television quickly replaced radio as the most popular form of entertainment.

An early television set. These TVs had small screens that only showed black-and-white images.

the decade of the 1940s began, the development of television slowed. When America became involved in World War II, RCA and other companies switched their focus to the war effort. So they put TV on the back burner.

## Early Television Sets and Shows

At war's end, however, this situation suddenly reversed. Many Americans now had the money to buy novelty items and they were clearly interested in purchasing TVs. In response, in 1945 and 1946 several companies began selling television sets for home use. At least six thousand were sold in 1946. Only a year later, the number had reached forty-four thousand. And by July 1948, 350,000 American homes had TVs.

These early commercial television sets were primitive by today's standards. The screens were small. And the images they carried were in black and white. Also, very few programs existed. Today, people take for granted many TV networks and stations, all running programs around the clock. In the late 1940s, however, only two networks—NBC and CBS—were broadcasting TV programs.

Moreover, these networks put out only a few hours of programming a day. In 1948 each had a fifteen-minute news program in the early evening. Each network also carried a few short entertainment programs in the late afternoon and evening. (The rest of the day and night they were off the air and viewers could see only static on their screens.)

## Early Children's Shows

Among the more popular of these early shows were those aimed at children. Especially big was the *Howdy Doody Show*, which began broadcasting in December 1947. Most of the characters on the show, including Howdy, a red-haired boy with freckles, were puppets. The creator of the show,

Television personality Buffalo Bob Smith poses with his puppet Howdy Doody. Smith's *Howdy Doody Show* was one of the first television shows for children.

Buffalo Bob Smith, played games and engaged in adventures with the puppets. It was the first network children's show to run five days a week. *Howdy Doody* was also the first TV show to run for more than one thousand episodes.

Another popular puppet show, *Kukla, Fran, and Ollie*, appealed to both children and adults. A real woman, Fran, talked to and sang with puppets Kukla and Ollie. In 1949, *Life* magazine wrote, "It is a children's puppet show whose audience is about 60 percent adult. . . . Its charm lies in the [very believable way in] which the show's creator . . . Burr Tillstrom, has endowed his hand [puppet] characters [with life]."[11] The characters were so believable, in fact, that when Kukla blew his nose one day on the theater curtain, more than 250 fans mailed handkerchiefs to the TV station.

## TV's Tremendous Potential

The most popular TV shows for adults were variety programs that featured comedy and music. One of these proved to be the first true megahit television show. In 1948 comedian Milton Berle launched the *Texaco Star Theater,* highlighted by his crazy, slapstick comic antics. Nearly every TV set in America tuned in once a week to see Berle walk into doors and take pies in the face.

As it turned out, Milton Berle did more than simply draw an audience. He was the first TV personality actually to create one. As the months rolled by, people across the country rushed out to buy TV sets just so they could see Berle's show. As a result, by August 1949 there were more than 2 million sets in the country. That was six times as many as existed only one year before. It is no wonder that Berle became known as "Mr. Television."

Only then, in the last few months of the decade, did America begin to wake up to the tremendous potential of television. Companies that made TV sets could barely keep

A family gathers around their television. By 1949 millions of televisions had been sold and stores had trouble keeping enough sets on the shelves.

up with the demand. (Twelve million sets had been sold by 1951.) Manufacturers of all kinds scrambled to advertise their products to the growing home audience. And to keep up with the demand for more programming, new TV stations appeared in every city.

It was now clear that television was going to become one of the biggest entertainment and money-making industries in America. It was also in the process of changing American culture. More and more people would get their news from TV and buy the products they saw advertised there. Also, the shows the baby boomers watched would shape their views of life and the world. Thus, the 1940s saw the important transition from the World War II generation to the first TV generation.

# Notes

## Chapter One: The United States Fights World War II

1. Quoted in Richard Hofstadter, ed., *Great Issues in American History: A Documentary Record, vol. 2, 1864–1957.* New York: Vintage, 1960, p. 392.
2. Quoted in Hofstadter, *Great Issues in American History,* pp. 403–406.
3. Mitsuo Fuchida and Masatake Okumiya, *Midway: The Battle That Doomed Japan.* Annapolis: Naval Institute Press, 1955, p. 29.
4. President Franklin D. Roosevelt, speech delivered to a joint session of Congress on Monday, December 8, 1941, in Diane Navitch, ed., *The American Reader: Words That Moved a Nation.* New York: Harper-Collins, 1990, p. 284.

## Chapter Two: America Emerges as a Superpower

5. Quoted in William Manchester, *American Caesar: Douglas MacArthur, 1880–1964.* London: Arrow Books, 1979, p. 400.
6. Quoted in Roger Bruns, *Almost History: Close Calls, Plan B's, and Twists of Fate in American History.* New York: Hyperion, 2000, pp. 65–66.
7. Quoted in Louis L. Snyder, *The War: A Concise History, 1939–1945.* New York: Dell, 1960, p. 596.
8. Quoted in John Costello, *The Pacific War.* New York: Rawson, Wade, 1981, p. 591.

## Chapter Three: Music Makes Its Mark on American Culture

9. Quoted in George Simon, *Glenn Miller and His Orchestra.* Cambridge, MA: De Capo Press, 1988, p. 217.

## Chapter Four: Television Captures the American Imagination

10. Quoted in Mitchell Stephens, "History of Television," *Grolier Encyclopedia.* www.nyu.edu.
11. *Life,* "Kukla, Fran, and Ollie," May 23, 1949, p. 17.

# Glossary

**blockade:** To stop commerce or traffic from moving into or out of a place. To keep a place isolated and contained.

**ensemble:** A group.

**humiliation:** Extreme embarrassment and/or shame.

**hydrogen bomb:** A nuclear weapon that works by the process of fusion. Atoms of hydrogen are forced together so violently that they turn into a heavier element, helium, releasing huge amounts of energy in the process.

**improvise:** To invent or make up something as one goes along.

**isolated:** Separated or cut off from the everyday world.

**jukebox:** A special vending machine that plays records when someone puts money in it.

**melody:** A clearly recognizable and usually pleasing tune in a song or other musical piece.

**radioactive elements:** Substances, such as radium and uranium, that are unstable and give off streams of micro-scopic particles (radiation).

**ration:** To limit or restrict the amount of something that people can have and use.

**78 rpm records:** Records that spin on the turntable of a phonograph at a rate of seventy-eight times per minute. Each side of such a record holds about three minutes of music.

**suburbs:** Tracts of houses, schools, and stores lying on the outskirts of cities.

**swoon:** To faint or fall down from excitement or delight.

# For Further Exploration

**Books**

Marion Calabro, *Zap! A Brief History of Television*. New York: Simon and Schuster, 1992. A lively, fact-filled introduction to the development of television, written for young readers.

Doreen Gonzales, *The Manhattan Project and the Atomic Bomb*. Berkeley Heights, NJ: Enslow, 2000. An easy-to-read summary of the Manhattan Project, the secret American effort to develop an atomic bomb during World War II and the effects of the weapon when it was used against Japan, ending that war.

Caroline Lazo, *Harry S. Truman*. Minneapolis: Lerner, 2002. The story of the president who guided the United States through the last days of World War II and the immediate postwar years.

Tom McGowen, *The Attack on Pearl Harbor*. Danbury, CT: Childrens Press, 2002. An effective description of the famous Japanese assault on the American fleet in Hawaii in December 1941, the event that drew the United States into World War II.

Don Nardo, *Franklin D. Roosevelt: U.S. President*. New York: Chelsea House, 1996. An easy-to-read volume that summarizes the life, struggles, and incredible accomplishments of one of the nation's greatest leaders, including how he guided the nation through the crisis of World War II.

Diane Yancey, *Life in a Japanese American Internment Camp*. San Diego: Lucent Books, 1998. Focuses on one of the darker episodes of American involvement in World War II. Out of fear that they would help the enemy, the U.S. government imprisoned Japanese Americans in concentration camps located inside the United States.

## Websites

**Big Band and Jazz Hall of Fame** (www.jazzhall.org). An excellent site that traces the history of American jazz, including blues, swing, bebop, rhythm and blues, and much more.

**Glenn Miller** (www.glennmillerstore.com). Contains links for various information on one of the leading figures of the Big Band era, including his biography and his music.

**North Harris Montgomery Community College District** (http://nhmccd.edu). An excellent site found at Kingwood College Library includes dozens of links to short, informative articles about different aspects of the 1940s. Highly recommended.

**PBS/WHGH Online** (www.pbs.org). An easy-to-read overview of how the United States and Soviet Union developed nuclear weapons in the 1940s and 1950s.

# Index

# Picture Credits

# About the Author

Historian and award-winning author Don Nardo has written many books for young people about American history, including *The American Revolution, The Mexican-American War, The Declaration of Independence,* and biographies of Presidents Thomas Jefferson, Andrew Johnson, and Franklin D. Roosevelt. Mr. Nardo lives with his wife, Christine, in Massachusetts.